For Gerry ~
more than likely
you have one or t...
dangerous women i...
family,
Pea...
Sept. 2022

Dangerous Women

Poems by
Jennifer Grant

BLUE LIGHT PRESS ◆ 1ST WORLD PUBLISHING

BLUE LIGHT PRESS
1ST WORLD
PUBLISHING

SAN FRANCISCO ◆ FAIRFIELD ◆ DELHI

Winner of the 2021 Blue Light Book Award

Dangerous Women

BLUE LIGHT PRESS
www.bluelightpress.com
bluelightpress@aol.com

1ST WORLD PUBLISHING
PO Box 2211
Fairfield, IA 52556
www.1stworldpublishing.com

BOOK & COVER DESIGN
Melanie Gendron
melaniegendron.com

COVER ART
"Aquarian Dream" by Melanie Gendron

AUTHOR PHOTO
Steve Douglas

FIRST EDITION

Library of Congress Cataloging-in-Publication Data

ISBN: 978-1-4218-3714-7

FOR MY MOTHER

*I don't think there is any place in the world
where a woman can't venture.*

– Ynes Mexia

Table of Contents

The Dowager of Light

Key West, 1832

For Lighthouse Keeper Barbara Mabrity

1.

I haul my fevered grief
up 88 spiraling steps.
For six years we two kept
the same dawn and dusk routine –

Fifteen lamps we lit nightly,
each reflector disassembled daily.
We filtered out the whale oil
and scoured each container.

I held light in my palms then,
polished all with a cotton crawl
before darkness fell atop
this 85-foot brick Cyclops.

Tonight, as I reach the final stair,
I wonder,
will my howling reach your ears?

This spit of land has laid claim to all that I am:
windblown, widowed woman with six children.
Half of my progeny still requires mothering,
the other three have their own young to tend.

Michael, you requested this post,
miles from my mainland family.
Far flung in the Florida Straits,
full of Judas Lanterns just like you.

How could you leave me!

2.

I look out over turquoise water –
the sea is dead with calm.
An iciness lingers in my fingers;
I sense something's wrong.

Three years I've tended
this lighthouse on my own;
watched paired pelicans flit
in flawless skies as one.

My lone mission now,
to keep mooncussers at bay
and sailors safe from reefs.

I'm told
the ocean's an angry woman
who churns and worsens
as each new squall rises.

I see myself more as a gale –
the ill-tempered tempest
who blusters her infinite fury.

I'm a no-name hurricane
who knows when to hunker down
and wait out ungodly gloom.

My cyclone of woe
continues for you Michael,
like this incoming storm.

Barnum Hotel Presents

The Spiritualist Sisters
New York, 1850

We sisters: Leah, Kate and Maggie
whisper secrets of wayward souls,
taste their acrid words on our tongues.

We Foxes, *Spiritual Knockers of Rochester*,
perform our specter-speaking show
three times today – 10 a.m., 5 p.m. and 8.

Like Destiny's deities,
we spin silken filament,
legends measured then snipped.

Unlike the grave Three Fates of Greece,
or those Roman grape crushers of hope,
we do not choose whose life begins or ends.

We simply chatter with the dead –
decipher rapping and tapping in walls,
offer messages from the Great Beyond.

Ignore that Northern Spy apple attached to string,
bumping along two-by-four floorboards and doors.
We're not banging knuckles or toes under tables.

We haunted three are touched by ghouls –
a dash of demonic delusion blended in our blood,
so mourners may buy low-cost solace.

Come sit in séance with us – circle round, clasp our hands.
We'll darken the parlor, reveal our vision of two years ago,
when a deceased peddler rattled bones in our Hydesville cellar.

Pay no mind to our little girl giggles
and overlook our odd occult origins,
which occurred on the Eve of Fools.

Whaling Wife

Sarah Parker Taber Boards the Alice Frazier

New Bedford, Mass.,
Sept. 10, 1851

1.

The wind slaps at their braided hair
and I grip both my girls' shaking hands.
I lift my chin toward the slate grey sky,
offer a swift moment of silent prayer.

We shall never again
wait three years
for our returning seaman.

In Spring, Daniel drifted home,
death rattling in his chest.
Chained to our marital bed,
he convalesced two months.

A delirious oath he whispered then.
But once his cough subsided,
waves and whale oil beckoned him.

We will not be left onshore
to wallow and wade through
another Winter's frozenness.

Daniel does not believe any mother
should endanger her daughters –
sailing the watery world
with 35 iron men in this wooden ship.

Asenath, Emily and I have sailor-strong souls.
We shall learn the ways of spades and harpoons:
along with steward, greenhands and coopers,
cooks, mates and my spouse.

Lord, bless this vessel –

On this hen frigate,
we shall float free
in high seas domesticity.
We shall succeed
or perish together.

2.

My penmanship is clearer,
so I rewrite Daniel's ship log.

For six months my pencil has etched,
re-created our daily sea life.

I doodle images in the margins
depicting what's been caught, or seen –
sperm whales, gulls, even octopi.

Today I'm too preoccupied to draw,
a gamming session's planned
for my silver birthday celebration.

Daniel will strap me into a basket
and hoist me to a neighboring ship
where society and poetry will congregate.

Captain Weir's wife and I will share
recipes we've concocted for healing,
seasickness, fleas, scabies and scurvy.

Emily, my salvation,
will scout for whales
while the crew recovers from drink.

Asenath, who has my penchant
for parchment and poems,
will enact her chosen words
as the sun slides into the sea.

3.
Our oddly tacked-together family
skims, navigates and cruises.
We keep the deck pristine
until it's covered in blood or blubber.

Despite our arduous labor,
my girls and I have velvety hands
from whale soap we've created.

We still cannot bear to watch
the brutal stabbings, nor the hauling.
We three sit, pray, or sing
in our quarters when it begins.

Death thumps the deck.
Dear Lord, do I dare admit
it's better than life in New England?

A Soldier's Secret Battle
Alexandria, VA
April 15, 1865

For Maria Lewis

1.

Church bells clang the saddest song –
The president is dead. The president is dead.

Lincoln's life's been snuffed
by a pistol-wielding actor.
I witnessed my first assassination
on that awful tobacco plantation.

As usual, I sit alone by a fading fire,
fingers steepled in private despair.
With Lincoln's passing,
maybe I should surrender my charade.

Two years ago, I escaped a master
and joined the Union Army Cavalry.
My emancipation passion led me
to a freedom run with 2,000 men.

We'll fight
for liberty till we die –

I've stolen these words and a character
from Harriet Beecher Stowe,
officially christening myself George Harris.
I'm my own hero from *Uncle Tom's Cabin.*

2.

When I first presented myself as a man,
no one stopped or ever examined me.

I grew accustomed to a soldier's world:
eating pasty gruel, swinging a sword
and never dressing near the men.

I got careless.

In a forest perfumed with white pine,
a lonely lieutenant confronted me.
He said my demeanor reminded him
of someone he missed at home.
As he backed me into a large hemlock tree,
I prepared to shoot and flee.

Instead of brandishing a whip,
lieutenant pushed his penmanship at me.
The looped words contained his sister's name
and Virginia residence.

3.

I understand the Army offers
no home for me as a woman.
But if I were a man, I'd commit
as long as breath stayed in my body.

I've endured battle-bruises in servitude and war.
The lieutenant's abolitionist sister Julia
declares my sacrifice deserves more
than *a new petticoat and hoops.*

Survival is three quarters luck.
Many more women exist like me,
whose femininity may never be set free.

Tears gush geyser-like from my eyes
for the first time –
Not just for Mr. Lincoln
but all souls who have perished.

Maybe like Beecher Stowe's George,
I shall sail to France and study at university.
Or maybe I will merely slip away and marry.
History is about men, after all.

Maria Mitchell's First Day
Teaching Astronomy at Vassar
Fall 1865

For Mary Fairfax Grieg Somerville and Maria Mitchell

To remind my girls of our lineage,
I lug Mary F.G. Somerville's plaster presence
up the steps to my classroom observatory.

You, reigning Queen of Science,
unallowed through closed doors after dark.
And I, wide-eyed American dreamer
of night skies and shooting stars
whose gazing discovery landed a job.

If I trace our trajectory –
we two comets, fiery creatures born to soar,
not submit to motionlessness.
We're both captivated
by the continuity of rotating planets
and shiny constellations.

You have a partner, a Mr. Somerville,
supporter of your celestial pursuits.
As I remain uncommitted,
Father and I will traverse the universe
from my third-floor telescope laboratory.

You and I share a first name –
mine, the Latin form of yours,
Christ's mother as well as Magdalene.
Are we beloved, rebellious,
or a dram of both?

You, with a Scottish uncle
who taught you to sailor-swear;
and my Nantucket tongue's salty whaler-flair.

When I was 12,
I started counting solar seconds for Father
from a rooftop during the eclipse of 1831.

All while you focused hours
on your *Mechanism of the Heavens* –
even diagramming motions of the moon!
You illuminated algebraic equations,
translating them into unpretentious language.
You, Mistress of Description,
gained royal entry
into the all-male Astronomical Society.

Three decades later,
I'm first woman in the states
paid as stargazing college professor.

Still, parents persist in governess requests –
that I survey their daughters daily
for curls out of place.
Is it my role to confirm or deny
whether my girls glide campus grounds
with affability and betrothal grace?

These knowledge-starved young ladies
will learn how to sweep
and measure a night sky,
using navigational chronometers, sextants
and their God-given minds.
They'll name all the stars
and comprehend planetary placement,

track and maybe uncover a comet –
like I did from the roof
of Pacific National Bank in 1847.
They'll also be tutored
concerning your *magnetic properties paper*
on violet rays of the solar spectrum.

I pray someday my students
will conceive not only future children
but a new universal order.

Until then,
I'll place your bust
in the center of my class –
our sun to revolve around.
I'll tell each woman:

Study as if you were going to live forever;
live as if you were going to die tomorrow.

Peak Performance

Lucy Walker, First Woman to Summit the Matterhorn, Considers Writing a Letter to her Rival, Marguerite C. Brevoort

Somewhere on the Swiss-Italian Border
July 22, 1871

I reached the apex, dear Meta –
4,478 meters up the Matterhorn pyramid.
First lady scaler in my ankle-length,
flannel-print dress.

Yes, I know your desire to mountaineer
sporting gentlemen's trousers.
But to me, femininity precedes divinity.

So close to the clouds,
I feel pulled toward prayer
and wish to reach the Almighty's ear.
I fall to my knees in exhausted gratitude.

My rheumatism remains oblivious.
That Liverpool doctor anticipated
I'd break bones rather than records.
A dozen years ago he prescribed walking
and growing my own root vegetables.
Rumors exaggerate my surviving
on champagne and chocolate cake.

You attended convent school in Paris,
so you understand outlandish stories.
And courting questions about why
we climbing ladies do not marry.
I respond thusly:

Since age 23 I have loved only two things –
alpinism and my long-suffering guide.
Thankfully, Melchior's already married.
I stay devoted to this spinsterhood!

We mountaineers pursue freedom and space,
wriggling up rocks and craving crisp open air.
We witness life from heaven's perspective.
How lovely that you commune with earth and sky,
along with your sweet dog Tschingel and your nephew.
My father and brother always accompany me.

My apologies for scrambling to finish first, Meta.
Two years ago you almost ascended,
before that maelstrom of blizzard and avalanche.
I knew then what I would do for snow-capped glory.

Zermatt's a tittle-tattle village
where secrets sweep in like winter wind.
I gathered my team when I heard whispers
of an attempt by *That American…*

Someday we shall sit together,
sip tea (or sparkling wine)
and revel in our adventures.

Prospecting with Husband
Dease Creek, Northern B.C.
February, 1874

For Nellie Pioche Cashman

1.

Disappearing is simpler in Winter,
when snow veils around my head.

Laden in heavy trousers
and chunky rubber boots,
I lean into the chill.

Boots are slow but better than snowshoes,
as ice often softens into a murderous slosh.

Even old McCullough, that noble discoverer,
succumbed a year ago in a foul weather white-out.

This morning the air tastes dry.
I blink, try to water my eyes.

I take a rickety breath,
blow circles of smoke.

Husband barks.
My hand-sled jerks.

I squint and look
toward dozens of wooden stakes,
saluting soldiers prepared for freshets
and searchers of riches, like me.

2.

I remove the pickax and toss it from my pack,
lean over the stream with cradle in gloved hands.

There are two types of deposits –

A lode imbeds in rocks,
impossible to reach
in unyielding ground.

I prefer placers,
metallurgic gifts,
settlers of riverbeds.

Rocking back and forth,
I sift, roll and screen a drenched pile.
Imagine stones sodden in gold.

No more boarders would I feed;
no more suitors would I need.

A sudden biting, blistering,
oven-hotness in my limbs
stirs me from gilded bliss.

I've over-stayed.
I whistle for Husband.
Where is that dog?

A Feminine First for Funambulism
Maria Spelterini Crosses Niagara River
July 12, 1876

A bored crowd now
means no money tomorrow.

I strap a pair of peach baskets to my feet,
wobble as I rise, shake my wiry red head.

The first step is a test.
I take a deep breath,
bend my knees to begin.

Robed in mist and roaring rapids,
wind whisks an *Ooooooh* to my ears.

With a balancing pole,
I implore the onlookers.

I'm two hundred feet below the bridge –
Wives wave white handkerchiefs,
husbands gesture with tall, inky hats.

Today's show has me
on two-and-a-quarter-inch wire,
stretched taught across the gorge.

Measuring exactly one thousand feet,
I need an equal amount of masculine
poundage to hold the cable down.

Halfway across, I feign a fall,
slight lean toward the rocky shore.

There's no fumbling in funambulism.
Precision takes months of preparation.

A danger artist creates drama
with at least a dozen daring acts.

Short skirts shudder as I inch forward.
A tiny hip wiggle realigns my spine.
I slip again and grin at the response.

Next attempt is blindfolded
and then backwards.
Maybe even manacled!

Hovering
between earth and air,
my refrain remains:
Amaze the masses.

Beckoning the Goddess

Trapped in a Tent During a Downpour, Archaeologist Jane Dieulafoy Prays to Nanaya in Susa, Persia

Spring, 1881

> *...Destiny does what it must for you – Rudaki, 10th Century*

May you, All Knowing Goddess of Love and War,
offer me the truth of Marcel's marriage equality oath.

He tells the men I'm more than his number one wife,
claims my betterment to four baby-bearing sisters.
I'm a digger, a writer and purveyor of antiquities.

May you, All Seeing Nanaya, glare upon Him
now that I realize my beloved's barbed lie,
sharply concocted to keep me body-bound.

Buttoned down in his shirt, baggy pants and long waistcoat,
I've even shaved off my lice-eaten hair and wear a pith helmet.

Oh Supreme Deity, who's privy to my petals of femininity,
now snoozing in the Zagros Mountain air.
May you anoint me, archaeology servant of your divinity.

Tomorrow, with whip on my hip and rifle on my shoulder,
the crew shall witness my strength exhuming your tomb.

My heart's aflame with stones of your pernicious past.
I pray in your name, my fate placed in your godly womb.

Drinking the Wind

Little Falls, N.Y.

Summer, 1886

For Mary Breed Hawley Myers

1.

Today we shall rise, Carlotta and I.
Her name handstitched in block letters
sky advertises our aerial exhibition.

Before Carlotta, I kept wifely records,
tested swaths of unusable fabric, sewed.

In my free hours I longed for clouds –

Surveyed thousands of flat stratus,
thick sun-blotting nimbostratus and
cauliflower-shaped cumulonimbus.

Before Carlotta, I could not fathom
floating forever with divine power,
a blinding light of lemon yellow
buoyed to my center.

I would rather drink the wind
than taste anything in this world.

2.

Four times dipped
in linseed oil and turpentine,
every pore of Carlotta's
pear-shaped body's baptized.

Under her open mouth
I sit on a thin wooden plank
suspended by hammock twine.

I tip my straw hat to the gaggle
below and a blast of air
steals it from my hand
when we hiccup.

I tap the barometer with my finger,
valve out the gas to slow us down.

Carlotta and I continue,
higher and higher.

A bolt of lightning
electrifies
the growling gray sky.

If her fabric fattens too fast,
my wingless angel will explode.

We must push on,
break through to heaven
where snow white cloudland emerges.

I am reborn.

No longer
Mrs. Carl Myers,
I am a lady aeronaut
nicknamed for my balloon,
The Carlotta.

A Sonata for the Valkyrie of the Piano

For Maria Teresa Gertrudis de Jesus Carreno Garcia de Sena

Berlin Philharmonic, 1889

1. Allegro

I'm misbehaving again –
performing the wrong opus.
My refusal stems
from hollow keys initiated by sterile men.
I will not propagate their infantile compositions,
glass shards shattering to the floor.

Husband Number 2 equates my moods
to our toddler's daily tantrums –
frenzied rages which lead
to nightly whiskey chasers.
I ignore his swilling librettos.

I'm known as Valkyrie quick –
with the rhythm of lightning
in all ten fingers.

Yes, I can be tempestuous,
like our family cat Chopin
who claws our cherry-colored curtains.
I shred through musical scores
until nothing remains.

Most men are not comfortable
engaging with ladies like me
whose dowry is finger electricity.

2. Adagio

At age 9, Papa made me play piano
onstage for American President Lincoln.
My recollection –
he was lanky as his black hat.
He touched my cheek and requested
I play *The Mocking Bird*, with variations.

Even then, my focus scaled
up and down 88 ebonies and ivories.
Papa always said my Venezuelan instinct
would prompt me when to slow my metronome down.

No such settling ever occurred.
I schooled myself as a mezzo-soprano.
My singular mission remained –
achieve international celebrity.

3. Minuet

If I had to choose,
Grieg would be my favored composer –
a Norwegian reminiscent of Odin.
As Valkyrie, I consider myself a helping spirit
to Edvard's godly wisdom and healing music.

But we Valkyrie are sinister,
using dark magic while flying below the clouds.
Just above the battlefield we handpick our deaths.
On the keyboard, I decide what sonatas survive
with flawless vigor and pianissimo agility.

Husband Number 3 keeps harping at me
that I do not pay attention to him or my six children.

4. Finale

Intermission awakens slumbering spouses –
along with their long-suffering wives,
they waddle to the lobby where they sip wine
and call each other sweetheart and darling.

I scoot backstage
and slip my aching hands into a bucket of ice.
My fingers, quivering skeletons.
I scream Odin's name in vain.

Oh Papa, if only you could have lived to see me.
Tonight is like my spotlight performance for Lincoln,
saucy girl draped in garlands of adoration.

I've become chooser of the slain,
an icon of feminine force.
And Husband Number 4 considers divorce.

I Do Confess

Annie Londonderry, First Woman to Cycle the Globe, Leaves Home

June 27, 1894

After William Carlos Williams' This is Just to Say

1.Boston, Mass.

I have stolen
your socks
that sleep in
our dresser.

Your favorite
woolen ones
worn only
in winter.

My apologies.
They are warm
and will keep
my feet pedaling.

Postcards
for our cherubs
shall follow
biweekly.

2. From Paris

I am the rage
for advertising –

A spot on my breast's
worth 100 francs!

Traded my bike
for one more lightweight.

I can do
anything
a man can.

3. From Arizona

Sorry specimen
of a tramp I am.

Someone stole my dress.
I now cycle in pants.

I know I was wrong
to leave you so long.

4. Getting Close

Two more days
until I make it
back home.

Your old socks
have more holes
than my heart.

Please meet me
and bring
our three children.

I promise –
no more cycling
or globetrotting.

Pearl Taylor Hart Spins the Mother of All Myths

Yuma Territorial Prison, 1899

> *Legends die hard. They survive as truth rarely does*
> *– Helen Hayes*

1.

In one tale I'm a wild-looking creature,
a furious storm of lightning and thunder.
In another I'm a devil with wide red eyes.
A third depicts me as clever and warm,
The Golden Fleece of summer.

Behind bars, men hold strange fascinations
with ghostly cowgirl legends.
Which western myth fits me?
May Agnes Fleming's *Queen of the Isle?*
Or, maybe dime novel *Duchess,*
wicked woman with a savage cry.

At birth, you monikered me Pearl,
after Botticelli's painter version –
Venus who rode an oyster shell.
You said I blew in on Zephyrus' wind,
but where's the Goddess of Spring,
awaiting me at the sandy shore?

From this damp jail cell I anticipate
a reporter whose wintery fountain pen
will whip me with a lesser nickname:

Bandit Queen
Lady Bandit

In the end,
I am just like you.

2.

Blind to the trappings of consummation,
at 16 I ran from your biblical upbringing.
I eloped with my first ne'er-do-well.
Low on cash, I used poverty as excuse.
In truth, I couldn't stomach his abuse.

Later, I latched onto a dance hall musician,
sang for suppers and pranced to Phoenix.
It wasn't until my music man vanished,
I cuddled up with Joe Boot –
who only adores his tarantula juice.

Then your letter arrived, Mama.
You were sick, as were both babies.
I pilfered cash from the saloon
and took money from lonely ranchers
who I wrangled with my wiliness.

Holding up one stagecoach yielded gold.
Don't shoot! I pleaded with Joe.
By dawn we two were caught,
sleeping by our dying fire.

Now I weave this tale to sell,
a legend to sew into my quilt of lies.
We mothers do what's required
to keep our children well and warm.

Burning Desire

Capt. Minnie Webb Leads Female Firefighters to First Call in Australia

For the Amazon Ladies Fire Brigade (1901-1905)

1.

A pinwheel of flame spins above me,
spitting sparks from the crystal chandelier.

Air hisses through cracked windows
and creaking within the walls warns me
this hotel could collapse, or explode.

I've trained for this pursuit since childhood:
it's what we've all dreamed of as career.
Leader of the Amazons, I'm a lady fire brigadier.

After I saw signal smoke, I was first on site.
I scrambled up the hotel's front steps,
in this gunny sack of a black dress –
a disastrous uniform that slows me down.

I can't see, nor breathe, through choking fog.
I bow my head, take measured shallow breaths,
as my Fire Chief Father taught all eight of us.

We're supposed to work in pairs,
but I've extinguished that demand.

2.

The alarm bells clang.
Must be Grace,
my second in command.

I screech for the water carriage.

Sisters May and Lily
haul and unroll the hose
fast as they can.

We all have our jobs.

My girls live to fight flames
alongside and equal to men.

That's why I ran toward today's blaze.
Not waiting around for brawny boys, or my team.

3.
Through a maze of thick soupiness
I scour every corner for survivors.

Nothing.

But I know there's someone.
It's a sense, like my father's.

A high-pitched scream.
A tiny angel flapping wings
in an oversized dressing gown.

I scoop her up
and flames lick my arm.

The doorway crumples.

I push toward the window,
smash it open with my elbow.

Trust me, I say.

Ada and Edith
will be ready with the canvas.
I cross my heart and we jump.

Death in the Afternoon

Wives, Daughters and Mothers React to La Reverte's Final Fight
Madrid, 1908

For Maria Salome Rodriguez Tripiona

La Reverte takes a bow,
bloody bull sprawled at her feet.

Dressed in a glittery cropped jacket
that blinks at us in the setting sun,
La Reverte lifts her chin skyward.

Manning a silk cape and sharp sword,
La Reverte has spent seven years
slicing through Spanish *corridas*.

Performing on tiptoes,
this dark-haired lady displays
ballets of feminine ferocity.

Today, we pile our applause
as high as the crimson roses.
Yet, La Reverte is unmoved.

We understand her attitude.
Our husbands, sons and brothers
call her a *marimacho* girl in pants.

La Reverte's accused
of causing matadorial confusion –
ignoring the decree that outlaws females
from competing with beasts in the ring.

In the end, instead of kisses,
she tosses a thick black wig
and bra padding to the dirt.

No!

We curse her from the stands
as La Reverte reveals
she's really a man.

Crowning Contemplation

Lady Bucking Horse Champion of the World Rises Before Dawn at Calgary Stampede
Sept. 2, 1912

For Fannie Sperry-Steele
After W.S. Merwin's "Little Horse"

Night before a bronc ride,
I always dream the same –

I'm six, running from
our white clapboard house;
screen door slaps shut.

Long brown mane flying,
green scarf waving in-hand,
I inhale the sunniness
of Mama's golden roses.

I wiggle my way
through the fresh-logged fence,
wink at Sleeping Giant Mountain.

I'm going to catch you for my own.

I slow toward the new colt,
loop my makeshift leash,
lasso the tike's willing neck.

We may as well kill it!
Papa don't like Pintos.

Protective pony parent,
I stiffen my stance.

Papa creeps up,
speaks low:

My Sperry Girls,
          'specially you Fannie,
a rare pedigree!

I nod.

He pats my head,
reassures I'm good
as any boy.

I awaken
drenched in sticky notions
of feminine imperfections.

Who wants to be
sweet as a chorus
of blueberry songs?

I'm a tad shadier,
a disfigured huckleberry
in my divided skirt.

Not gonna hobble my stirrups,
tie them together with a
cinch strap to secure myself.

Like any man,
I want to dismount
at first trace of trouble.

I slip on my boots,
wipe dream
from my eyes.

Time to tame
Red Wing.

Of Felines and Femininity

Circus Performer Rose Flanders Bascom's Birthday Song of Strength for her Child, 1915

> *The smallest feline is a masterpiece – Leonardo da Vinci*
> *You never can trust a cat – Clyde Beatty*

Male tamers compare female cats to fickle women
and choose larger and louder boy lions –
Oh, Agnes, those lazy kings of beasts
lounge nearly 20 hours each day.

Every truth gathered in this life
I've clawed from circus cats –
the swiftness of a leaping cheetah,
the loyalty of a tawny cougar.

Femininity can be a weapon of quiet ferocity.

Watch, Sweet Girl, how felines live –
black panther protecting her only cub,
puma's stealthy power.
Pay attention to quick cat moves.

In Contoocook, where I was raised,
native Pennacooks taught children
animal totems:
Jaguar as a shape shifter
and domestic cat as magical guardian.

Femininity is the witch-like wand
I learned to wield with felines on my side.

Never have I manned a whip
in my center-stage cage with Tippy;
I just listened close
to the snarling tone of that 200-pound kitty.

Let femininity be your weapon, Agnes,
and keep a feral tiger by your side.

The Wooing of Filmmaker Marion Wong

Creating *The Curse of Quon Gwon*

1916

Reel 1 – On a Ship Returning from China

I clutch camera and pen
in a drowning death dream.
It's not the Titanic
or last year's Lusitania.
Nonetheless, it's sinking.

Sloshing seas awaken me.
My singular hope refocuses –
I'd rather be deceased than betrothed.
I vow to be bound only to American film.

My parents stand in tandem,
overlords of my stateroom sickbed.
Worry twins their foreheads.
A double nod gifts this second daughter
exactly one year to raise a career.

Reel 2 – First Day of Hollywood Filming

Just like me, lotus and red tea
will never satiate the 30 Asian actors
I've collected like mahjong pieces.
Even Mother requests her own role.
She smirks at the cast when I shout *CUT.*

Little empress just needs a strong spouse.

I clench my teeth to prevent retort
and draw my lead actress aside.
Violet, my brother's wife,
plays a heroine truer than that vamp,
the big-eyed Theda Bara.

Heavy chains slipped around my wrists
are not so different than a marriage.

We two women crave apple pie
and the sweetness of marital modernity,
rather than the plum blossoms
important to our parents.

Reel 3 – Opening Night

Scores of family and fans flutter
from ticket booth to auditorium
while I give an hour-long interview
to a reporter with the *Oakland Tribune.*

I slink down,
a row behind my father.
Mother's seat is empty;
she's entertaining in the lobby.

If my parents could just realize
my silver screen ambitions
are not cursed, but well-rehearsed.
Distribution's cheaper than a dowry.

Hmph, Papa says.

Reel 4 – At Home, One Year Later

That Berkeley boy's at the door –
An electrical engineer
who understands my schematics
and whispers why we should marry.

I'll buy you a theatre.

My heart shutters.
The silence is deafening
as we fade to dark.

Suffragist or Mystic?
Komako Kimura Headlines Page One
New York, Aug. 1, 1919

1.

You name me the Mystic Healer of Japan,
even though it's my beloved who doctors.
I roll up my left sleeve,
pierce my skin with 10 tiny needles.
I ignore the ache in my abdomen.

I will my brain not to feel pain.
It's the shard of a lie I've refined to a pinpoint.
I weep with each evening's moon.

I will my body NOT to shed blood.
And as I will, so my body acts.

You scribble loops in your notebook
as if your fountain pen will quote me
with acupuncture precision.

My inky hair
reflected in your camera's eye:
a few silver strands shine,
errant pieces of the spider's web
I've weaved here in America.

2.

Two years ago, I marched New York
with women of all cultures and colors.
Garbed as geisha in a kimono –
purple lotus and green leaves
with a gold obi at my waist.

A mask of extra powder on my face,
I carried a flag in each hand –
left for land of the rising sun
and right for the stars and stripes.
Another performance with roots of truth.

3.

As I peer at the pins in my forearm,
You, Reporter Man, mention porcupines.
I nibble at a slit in my bottom lip.
It stings.

I will not articulate my unyielding love
for a divorced man,
how I bore our son outside of matrimony
and had to bury our baby girl.
This New True Woman
swallows her sincerities.

You need not know
my suffering.

I smile and nod.

Ode to the Stage Curtain

Esther Deer Prepares for First of 246 Performances in Broadway's *Tip Top*

1921

*Beauty, of course, is the most important requirement
and the paramount asset of the applicant – Florenz Ziegfeld*

The Great Globe Theatre is usually sprayed
with scorn and yellow headed wildflowers.

Today, embroidered pixies pull me on stage
and hope drapes my once chilled shoulders.

I'm wrapped and fireproofed,
adorned in flames of crushed red velvet.

Ziegfeld Girls begin and end in costume –
we premeditate postures and positions.

I take my mark, arch my back.

As the curtains shimmy open,
I realize I am barefooted.

Such a gaffe could have me moccasin-clad
and sheathed in animal skin by dawn;
left to drift with my family's rodeo show.

Quick to pivot, I squint and point.
I wiggle five toes toward hot footlights:
Just who of you stole my shoes?

The audience erupts into laughter
and I, Princess White Deer, ascend.

The Rules of Horse Diving

Savannah Fairgrounds, 1923

For the first Girl in Red, Lorena Carver

1.

I'm craning my neck to watch her –
a girl, 40 feet up on a whitewashed perch.
She's clad in a crimson swimsuit and rubber shoes.
Her face is shaded by a football helmet.

She waves to the gawking crowd,
ignoring her stomping mount.
This girl's forgotten the first rule:
The animal is always in charge.

I shake my head;
miffed I'm still lame.

I stick my hand in the tank, swish it around.
Water sloshes over the brim.
In this 10-feet of water, horse and girl will land.

I, myself, haven't performed in a year.
Just the thought makes me ornery,
especially today when Doc demanded
I secure an ad in the newspaper –

Wanted:
Attractive young woman
who can swim and dive.
Likes horses, desires to travel.
See Dr. W. F. Carver.

The sugarcane sweetness Doc seeks
makes my wisdom teeth ache.

I am a horse woman,
hailing from a cow town near Kansas City
where Doc started this equine exhibition.

I count to five and raise my arms.
The girl in red swivels and swings her legs
around the approaching horse's girdle.

At least this one leaps when told.

2.

I was barely 15 when I convinced Doc
to let me ride Klatawah for his shows.

I'd been practicing for months,
in the hours before hungover eyes
of wild west showmen peeled open.

Klatawah shared my philosophy.
Her name meant *go to hell, or go away,*
depending on my voice inflection.

She raised her brown plumed tail
and trotted up the rickety ramp toward the tower,
where I waited on the gate like a rodeo rider.

I measured her steps and heavy breaths
until her front hooves reached out to me.
I bowed, then slid my left side over her.
In the next moment we two fell free,
her mane and my hair comingling.

Doc found me soaked and smiling.
He yanked me from the icy water:
Keep your goddamn head tucked!

That became rule number two.

3.

Doc's hoping this Savannah girl
joins our travelling sideshow.
Her fluttery femininity
makes my brother Al pink cheeked.
He's usually pinched-faced
and prickly mouthed, like our father.

Both men offer soft words to pretty girls.

Al trains the horses, riders, and fills the water.
I organize and pay the bills.
And Doc, our dad, dictates the rules.

Even after those 32 stitches I endured
when I was kicked in the jaw
and the eight fractures in my arm
when I landed wrong.
I rode through piercing pain
while Doc kept screaming:
Hold tight, but loose!

Remembering the rules
is what remains and endures.
I mustn't forget that pail of oats
to reward today's starring horse.

Inventor Inspection

Lillian Tolbert Scans First Woman's World Fair Souvenir Program
Chicago, April 18, 1925

We are architects and actresses,
fox breeders and bookstore workers.

We are a compilation of costumers,
ceramic engineers, dressmakers
and designers of ladies' underwear.

A few equal employment experts
have slipped in – like me –
through the back and side doors.

It's a festival of femininity,
one hundred gender defying jobs
at the American Exposition Palace.

Here in booth number 22,
I butterfly my hands,
embracing my innovative ice pitcher.

Behold its mid-section:
A two-inch wide cylinder!

I shovel frozen cubes into its belly.
This contraption chills water, sweet tea,
and on dreary days, dry martinis.

I receive a couple of steely smiles
as one of the few women of color.
I float alone in this ghostly sea

of jewelers, keepers of kennels
and starch-faced law officials.

None of us ladies get paid
half the pennies of any male.

Oh, we opine optimism,
continuing to plumb pipes
and paint portraits quietly.

We recognize we're second class
to every sorry gentleman.
We are typecast as willful women.

Yet, the only man who participated
in my invention was an attorney
in the patent office!

We are unbridled visionaries.
We are seekers and makers
of small wonders.

And for a moment,
I am satisfied.

Powering Through

At Age Twenty, Trudy Ederle Attempts Second English Channel Swim

Aug. 6, 1926

Cape Gris-Nez, France - Dover, England

1.

Twenty-eight strokes per minute since dawn.
Halfway, I slow down –

                     Lose count.

Seven hours
I've chopped through seaweed,
fishing nets, even a doll's head.

My rubber bathing cap itches.
Amber tinted goggles fogged.
Can't feel my swollen tongue.

Pops spews orders from a tiny tug boat;
points toward a mass of ruby red jellyfish.

He strikes my elbow with a glass baby bottle.
My stomach lurches at the thought
of lukewarm chicken broth.

Big sis Meg tosses a turkey leg at my head.

The wind is rising.
The sky is crying.

Come out girl!

What for?

2.

Pain trickles down to my toes;
lungs heave with each lifted arm.

I hear songs of honking horns.
Am I closing in on Dover shore?

Dear Lord, It's too dark!

Keep counting each stroke.
Staying focused on my goal.

I'd rather drown than give up now.

St. Mary's Bay Lighthouse winks
a flashing prayer across the waves.

I take this as a divine sign.

Pull off your goggles!
Only 400 yards to go!

Is it God, or Pops screaming?
Either way, I do what I'm told.

The world breaks open
with bonfires and bobbling boats.

I swim harder.

I reach shore on all fours,
grasping for ground.

When I try to rise Pops runs
toward me with a robe in hand.

Stay Back!
I must stand on my own.

I wobble.
Someone yells the time.

It's 9:40 p.m.
Two hours faster than any man.

Ode to Mimosa Mexiae

Botanist Ynes Mexia Becomes Permanent Exhibit in Herbaria
of the World

1928

I am the specimen picked late,
placed in a yellowed pillowcase
and securely saddle-draped.

I am in the pea family – *Fabaceae*.

I'm sensitive to light and touch,
leaves drooping from over stimulus.
Muted independence, my prayer and solace.

Most mimosa consist of herbs or under-shrubs.
Some creepers, like me, pointed and prickly.
Others contain poisonous roots,
or irritate those with thin ivory skin.

Bountiful Botanist Joseph Nelson Rose,
surnamed for pale beauty with thorns,
you regale me by relabeling me *Mimosa*.

As tree, I'd explode in purple or pink stars,
create long silky threads of my own golden stamen.

I am hardy, yet wilt has occurred –
my leaves withering before midsummer,
ooze cracking through my near 60-year-old trunk.

You do not know of my two husbands –
one plucked by death, the other by divorce.
You're not privy to my decades searching,
unearthing love through soil raking therapy.

Today's rolling fog at dawn,
my redwood path briefly obscured.
Alone on this California trail,
heart revived by emerald floral walls –
corners to trowel and hills to climb.

On horse or on foot,
I aim to collect 100,000 species
worldwide before my demise.
I only have so much time.

The Girl Who Flirts With Death
Los Angeles, 1930

For Agnes Micek aka Lillian La France

1.

My bike growls
and rounds the 80-degree bank turn.
Speed lifts and eases me sideways.

When the crowd peers over the lip,
it's as if they too are spinning
at this 100-mile-per-hour-clip.

Welcome to the Murder Drome,
my sacred circle of high rolling.

Today's mile-and-a-quarter circuit
is a half-assed construct of 2-by-2 lumber.
If I spill? Imminent splinter impalement.

You've provided warnings –
those who cheated you
and then succumbed:

Eddie Hasha:
Lost control in Newark in 1912.
Shrimp Burns:
Terminal tumble in Toledo in 1921.
Ray Weishaar:
Crashed in the City of Angels in 1924.
And Eddie Brinck:
Smashed up in Springfield, Mass. in 1927.

You think I'm a girlish gambler?
I understand odds; it's all mathematical.
Plugging in the numbers
and not acting as a two-wheel
flying demon-man in the saucer.

Still want to snag me?
Not a chance.

2.

In the beginning I was Agnes –
Of God, of Rome.
Named for a chaste saint,
pure as priest water.

Images of martyred virgins nauseate –
my natal name "lamb" in Latin.
I would rather be slaughtered
than compared to sheepishness.

I've converted to Lillian,
not the devotional flower.
Donning a logo of skull and crossbones –
I'm The Matriarch of Motorcycles.
I'm the holy hellion winking at you.

Fast Woman

Sao Paulo Grand Prix, Brazil

1936

> *It's all I ever ask for, just to show what I can do*
> *without a handicap against men – Helle Nice*

1.

A mistake
on the race's last lap.
I overcorrect my Bugatti.

Shoddy brakes –
shaky, scrambled like my brain,
as my head slams the wheel.

I'm conscious
of blood from nose to mouth
but I refuse to slow my pace down.

I careen
toward the onlooking fans.
A sea of screams swims through my skull.

I stop hard.
Is it a wall, or man?
Oh God, I know the thud is human.

Smoke billows.
Flames rage around and within me.
The racetrack blackens as death gestures.

2.

A naive girl –
sixteen with starry dreams.
Paris painters expose my nude form.

Brokenness
cannot be avoided.
We females are fractured by mankind.

I beguile,
twirl my budding shape onstage.
I'm handblown glass before it hardens.

I splinter
as a crystal goblet.
The break caused by an avalanche.

I'm injured.
A smashed ski-knee cripples me,
so I piece together a car career.

3.

Awakened.
A whistling in my ears.
Tangled tongues track my hospital bed.

No support.
Unsmiling men blame me
for six deaths at the Grand Prix Raceway.

Flawed female.
I will not be destroyed.
Fast women are designed to endure.

Sky Writing

Pilot Tosca Trasolini Takes Popular Flying Magazine Editor to Task After First All-Day, All-Female Flight

November 1936, Vancouver Airport

For Jean, Betsy, Alma, Elianne, Margaret, Rolie and Tosca

You didn't see us drift all day in the open sky.
You didn't see us at sunset, land in amber air.

We dangerous women
blew in on borrowed wind.

We demanded masculine objectivity,
pushed through fog of feminine obscurity.
Our crew clad in leather flying hats,
each swore to wear tight gray lips.

A pair of Gypsy Moths, a couple of Fleets,
two Fairchildren and a soaring Golden Eagle:
all tail draggers with no mechanics required.

Our fathers told us to secure a spouse.
Our mothers told us to keep a clean house.
We promote neither, though three of us
chose husbands as well as wings for flight.

We're maiden mounters of clouds.
The open sky is where we belong.

Why did you dismiss us today?
We, the Vancouver Flying Seven,
women who transcended.

Cooking Up a Cross Creek Life

A Writer Reflects on Her Crab Newburg Recipe

1939

For Marjorie Kinnan Rawlings

Prep time (approx. 10 years) – This recipe begins with *Lima Beans*, a vegetable that takes longer to mature than green beans. It's also a University of Wisconsin stage show in which I had a role – my burgeoning affair with poaching, baking and braising words and food.

Ingredients

Yolks of 2 marriages – first one I deem rotten and toss, second is golden.
Center-strong yet mushy.

½ cup of heavy cream dreams to concoct at least one great American novel.

½ cup of salt springs – a place I gather crustaceans and an array of crusty characters.

2 snifters of sherry or madeira if social occasions arise, or workaday warrants it.

A pinch of cayenne – to uplift and reverse anguish over citrus crop loss and my hollow womb.

A pound of crab, Florida lobster, or even a de-feathered limpkin (that wetland forager who specializes in apple snails) as I am sand-pine needle close to *losing all sophistication and perspective* the longer I reside in this green and white cracker farmhouse in the Big Scrub.

Directions

In a tiny town in North Central Florida, named for a short stream connecting Orange and Lochloosa lakes, mix in two Wisconsin badgers turned newspaper reporters, adoration of soil, swampy seasons and a cropped kinship. Purchase a 72-acre frontier farm. It must be *off the beaten path* with mysterious palms, live oaks and *dripping with grey Spanish moss.*

Combine with days of scribbling and typing words for at least four books created on a table made of cypress boards and cabbage palm trunks. Prepare to slumber on an adjacent daybed when steamy afternoon humidity reaches its sweaty fingers through the screened porch windows. Add a dash of friendship with writers whose eyes are also watching God – I'm speaking of you, Zora Neale Hurston – and whip up a story of a boy becoming a man. Toss in a yearling. Gather a Pulitzer for the final meringue and *ta da*!

Serve all personal effects on a china platter to the University of Florida at life's end.

Unveiled: Memoirs of Harem Years in Cairo

Being a female became a barrier between me
and the freedom for which I yearned
– Huda Sha'arawi

1.

The taste of childhood
still lingers on my tongue –
pears and citrus, apricots and plums
all from Father's garden.

I open the curtain,
my first day as a woman.
After praying two *rakaas,*
bowing and prostrating
on a mat of red velvet.
After new husband lifted my silvery veil
and kissed my forehead.
I'm trembling, like a branch in a storm,
unable to reach for my goblet of red sorbet.

Now I peek out the window –
Barren. No nuptial tent. No flowers.
Father's blooming garden gone.

I plunk piano keys,
practicing my scales to create sound.
Husband huffs and puffs.
No words.
I cannot take much more.
He speaks: *Have you read it?*

I recollect an envelope inked:
To the Lady.
Thought it meant my mother.

I race to my old room,
rip through piles of papers.
One flutters to the floor,
stamped and signed by two witnesses.

My heart leaps when I understand
my spouse refuses to take any other wife.
Then: *His slave-concubine shall be freed.*
She and *their* babies will live with his mother.

I run away.
Ashamed. Angry. I am not sure which
since my wedding wasn't consummated.

2.

Saiza Nabarawi and I lock hands,
lift our veil-less faces toward the sun.
We're rallying ladies in the streets,
protesting to raise the betrothal age.

I was 13 the day Mother married me off
to a cousin three decades my senior –
she begged me to agree so he'd educate me.

I do not wish to complain,
as I learned to speak and read
French, Turkish and Arabic poetry.
But no girl should be wed
before her first moon's set.

Mother's passed;
as have Father, Brother and Husband.
Free of familial binds,
I now push forward

with my newest campaign:
No marriages until at least age 16!

Saiza and I vow
to tout this marital refrain
for females like my own delicate flower –
May my child and all Egyptian women retain
a strength as mighty as any Cairo train.

3.

My friend Saiza, who is more of a daughter,
edits news in a downtown building
now known as The House of Women.
She's busy steering *L'Egyptienne*
while I shuffle memoirs of my harem years.

I dictate to my secretary:
Fate mocks us and is cruel.

I've been decorated by the state
for toiling decades to shape femininity's future.
Saiza and I removed and waved our veils
after we attended the
International Women's Suffrage Alliance in 1923.
How will our feminist crusade conclude?
As it began, on this slow-moving train.

Despite our work for change –
the marital age,
women university graduates in 1933
and planting other seeds of equality,
there's still a long track to travel.
I'm overcome with exhaustion.

I refuse to sacrifice women's liberation
for men's political or personal ambitions.
Even with my own spouse!
Seven years I clutched my bitterness
and lived apart to protect my heart.
But in the end, he was my husband
and my duty included raising children.

My life will not remain hidden.
We who procured the reins of feminism –
from *Eugenie Le Brun,* whose salons
swayed and empowered us
as heroines of our own storytelling.
It's time to unveil our tales.

Acknowledgments

I've always been intrigued by courageous women in history who didn't follow societal rules as "ladies." In fact, my first published novel involved two female pirates. But it wasn't until I discovered *Careers of Danger and Daring,* by Cleveland Moffett, that I considered crafting a series of persona poems. The 1903 book concerned men, but I spotted a picture of "Mme. Carlotta" steering her husband's hot air balloon. That's all it took to fuel my obsession.

By no means is this a complete collection of incredible women from the 1830s-1940s. I offer a glimpse of lesser-known adventurers who shaped our modern world. Much of what I've written contains speculation. As truth tends to be stranger than imagination, I am grateful for the following books that provided time period tidbits: *Captain Ahab Had a Wife,* by Lisa Norling; *Courageous Women of the Civil War: Soldiers, Spies, Medics and More,* by M. R. Cordell; *Reflections of A Romantic Biographer,* by Richard Holmes; *Personal Recollections of Mary Somerville,* 1874; *Wild West Women,* by Rosemary Neering; *Young Woman & The Sea,* by Glenn Stout; *Death and Money in the Afternoon: History of Spanish Bullfight,* by Adrian Shubert; *In Search of Princess White Deer,* by Patricia O. Galperin; *A Girl and Five Brave Horses,* by Sonora Carver; *Cross Creek,* by Marjorie Kinnan Rawlings; *American Women Afield: Writings by Pioneering Women Naturalists,* edited by Marcia Bonta; and *Harem Years: The Memoirs of an Egyptian Feminist,* translated and introduced by Margot Badran.

First drafts of many of these poems were written during two Blue Light Press poetry workshops – Spring and Fall of 2019. That's why I am particularly honored to be a recipient of Blue Light Press' Book award for 2021.

I attended Palm Beach Poetry Festival's workshop in January 2020, working with Adrian Matejka and his studio of amazing poets. I followed up with online mentoring with San Francisco Poet Diane Frank. A couple pieces also bloomed during a 2020 Zoom workshop (Writers in Nature) with former Alabama Poet Laureate Sue B. Walker. I appreciate all the cheerleading to continue scribbling.

I would also like to thank my mother, for whom this collection is dedicated. She taught my sister and me strength and the importance of independence, but to love with our entire beings. My writer son, Sam, was indispensable in this book's creation. He read each poem in its infancy and offered insightful edits. Poet Robbie Curry kept me inspired when I floundered, and Jessica K.M. Rascovich required "woman-of-the-week" updates. And finally, I'd like to thank my beloved, Tim, who has embraced my somewhat dangerous nature for more than three decades. I adore you.

About the Author

Jennifer Grant resides in Newberry, Florida. *Dangerous Women* is her second collection of poetry. Her first, *Good Form*, was published by Negative Capability Press (2017) and a tiny chapbook, *Bronte Sisters and Beyond*, through Zoetic Press (2018). Her chapbook *Year of Convergence* was included in Blue Lyra Press' Delphi Series Vol. IX (2020). Find out more at jenniferlynngrant.com.

CPSIA information can be obtained
at www.ICGtesting.com
Printed in the USA
LVHW030515290122
709518LV00001B/17